Today is the first day of the rest of forever. How are you going to spend it? For starters, we suggest reading Dick Eastman's informative *Cram Course for Eternity*. It's about a matter of life or death. Your life or death.

CRAM COURSE FOR ETERNITY

DICK EASTMAN

Whitaker House
504 LAUREL DRIVE, MONROEVILLE, PA 15146

©Copyright 1972 by Dick Eastman
Printed in the United States of America
0-88368-047-5

All rights reserved. No portion of this book may be used in any form without the written permission of the publisher, with exception of brief excerpts in magazine articles, reviews, etc.

Scripture quoted is from *The Living Bible,* Tyndale House Publishers, used by permission.

Excuse Me . . .

. . . could I talk with you for a few seconds? It's about something that will revolutionize your life. And I know what you're thinking: "Somebody's trying to push religion down my throat again."

But hold on a minute. It's true, I do want to share Jesus with you. But I'm not trying to sell you anything. I'm not trying to start a movement. And I'm not trying to make money. Jesus said, "freely ye have received, freely give."

The fact is, Jesus isn't a gimmick. Jesus Christ is more than a button or a bumper sticker, or passing the offering plate. Jesus is Life. And Jesus is in the business of changing people, of offering them a new kind of living that starts the minute they decide they want it to, and lasts for all eternity.

Oh, you can laugh it off if you want to; some do. But this decision will be your life's most important. What you decide will determine how you spend forever—starting right here, right now. If you'll set just a moment aside to take a *Cram Course for Eternity*—and take it honestly—I can show you how to pass the biggest test you'll ever have to take with flying colors. And I promise that you'll never be the same!

DICK EASTMAN

Contents

1. The Searching Factor 9
2. The Father Factor 15
3. The Son Factor 21
4. The Spirit Factor 27
5. The Truth Factor 33
6. The Lordship Factor 39
7. The Prayer Factor 45
8. The College of the Word 51

the searching factor

Hypothesis One—Sooner or later in life everyone finds himself asking three basic questions: (1) Who am I? (2) Why am I here? and (3) Where am I going?

Cram Course for Eternity

I chuckled a little when I heard the joke about the long-haired drop-out who traveled the world searching for himself. Then one day he cut his hair, and there he was.

But now I don't laugh quite so hard. Unfortunately, there's a whole generation of youth (and adults) who can't seem to find their reason for being. Some even wonder if they're for real. Most really can't tell you why they are here. And the majority have no answer for where they are going. The old Beatle ballad, "Nowhere Man," seems to smack them in the face with truth. Like the man in the song, they feel as though they, too, are making all their "nowhere plans for nobody."

Youth who joined the revolutionary movement of the sixties have deserted it, except for a feeble few. Several once-avid "movement" admirers were recently interviewed. One candidly commented, "I got disgusted—the last peace meeting I went to turned into a fist fight."

Another openly declared, "I tried for two years and saw it impossible to change things." The third simply looked the reporter in the eye and said, "I lost faith."

And that's the picture of people today. A whole generation has lost its faith. They can't even find happiness or meaning in the dollar bill anymore. Remember actress Judy Garland? Her daughter, Liza Minnelli, re-

Cram Course for Eternity

cently spoke of her once wealthy, once popular—even once alive—famous mother. One line from that interview left me shocked. Liza shared, "She (Judy Garland) had a good life, she had fun. Everything was like an enormous party." As you may know, Miss Garland tried more than once to take her life. Of these attempts Liza Minnelli says, "They were silly, half-hearted but glamorous."

The last attempt, however, lacked what I would call glamor. It sent the middle-aged actress to her grave. And I somehow can't agree with the philosopher Camus who said, "Suicide is prepared within the silence of the heart, as is a great work of art."

Life *can* be more than just "one enormous party." Parties seldom provide peace. You won't find happiness in dope-peddling friends or in crisp dollar bills. And that goes for adults, too. (It's not just youth who are sometimes hung-up on material things.) No matter what your age or status in society is, you simply cannot buy peace and happiness with money. Andrew Carnegie laid it on the line: "Wealth lessens rather than increases human happiness. Millionaires who laugh are rare."

So I've reached a conclusion in my human experience. No matter where I travel I notice one factor prevalent in people of all races and nations. It's the searching factor.

Cram Course for Eternity

Everyone, even the person with "everything," asks at least one of these basic questions: Who am I? Why am I here? Where am I going?

That's the reason for this *Cram Course for Eternity*. On the pages following we will answer these questions. We will share what the Bible says concerning genuine peace and a reason for living. We will explain how you can involve yourself in the Jesus life and be changed forever. So don't stop reading now. Come along and experience this exciting life for yourself.

Cram Course for Eternity

What's Your Opinion?

Before reading what the Bible says concerning hypothesis one, check this simple questionaire. Do it in your spare time. After completing it ask yourself why you answered as you did.

1. When I woke up this morning I . . .
a. ☐ found myself to be at perfect peace.
b. ☐ found I dreaded facing the day.
c. ☐ found myself wishing I were dead.

2. At this point in my life I . . .
a. ☐ definitely know my reason for being.
b. ☐ sometimes feel I have little direction.
c. ☐ don't really know why I am alive.

3. In looking at tomorrow I . . .
a. ☐ am thrilled with all the prospects.
b. ☐ don't think that far into the future.
c. ☐ am miserable just thinking about it.

4. In discussing life in general I . . .
a. ☐ know there is a God-given plan for me.
b. ☐ question things about God's existence.
c. ☐ absolutely don't believe in God.

Now go back and think about your choices!

The Bible Says . . .

"For I know the plans I have for you," says the Lord. "They are plans for good and not for evil, to give you a future and a hope. In those days when you pray, I will listen. You will find me when you seek me, if you look for me in earnest" (JEREMIAH 29:11-13).

"Since earliest times men have seen the earth and sky and all God made . . . they knew about him all right, but they wouldn't admit it . . . the result was that their foolish minds became dark and confused" (ROMANS 1:20;21).

"Let me say this, then, speaking for the Lord; Live no longer as the unsaved do, for they are blinded and confused. Their closed hearts are full of darkness; they are far away from the life of God because they have shut their minds against him, and they cannot understand his ways" (EPHESIANS 4:17, 18).

"Don't let others spoil your faith and joy with their philosophy, their wrong and shallow answers built on men's thoughts and ideas, instead of on what Christ has said" (COLOSSIANS 2:8).

COMING UP NEXT . . .
Is There Really A God?

the father factor

Hypothesis Two—There exists in the universe a God. He is a person who created everything. He is the essence of real love. He is all-powerful and all-knowing. He is not a myth. He exists. The whole universe speaks on behalf of His existence.

Cram Course for Eternity

An account comes to mind that I shared in my book *Up With Jesus*. A teen-ager had come into my office to discuss the question of God. He called himself an "agnostic" and saw little reason to believe in God.

I asked pointedly, "Would you agree that the chair you are sitting in was manufactured by a chair company?" He nodded affirmatively.

"Would you further agree that this desk was built by someone who had knowledge of desk design?" I asked. He agreed without question. He also agreed that the carpet was manufactured by someone familiar with carpet weaving.

Then I questioned, "In looking at the trees and grassy hillsides, or the complexities of our human bodies, are we wrong to assume there is a supreme Designer?" He responded bluntly, "I don't think that proves anything."

What an answer! I quickly fired back, "Do you mean that the mere existence of a chair, carpet, and desk is evidence to you of a human designer; yet you recognize no designer of far more complex objects?" The lad was stunned. And not long after, he changed his belief. He soon believed in God and received Christ as Lord of his life.

Where on earth did that ridiculous trend begin anyway? I mean the idea that there is no God. It had to come from the hearts of

Cram Course for Eternity

rebellious men who just didn't want to obey God. The idea certainly couldn't have originated from common sense. Look around. Absolute logic speaks for a God. No wonder the Bible never tries to prove God, it just says He always existed.

I recently picked up a pamphlet titled *There Is No God?*[1] It began, "There is no God . . . all the wonders around you are accidental. No almighty hand made a thousand billion stars. They made themselves. No power keeps them on their steady courses. The earth magnetized itself to keep the oceans from falling off toward the sun." The piece went on to declare, "Infants teach themselves to cry when they are hungry or hurt. A small flower invented itself so that we could extract digitalis for sick hearts. The inexhaustible envelope of air—only fifty miles deep, and of exactly the right density to support human life—is just another law of physics."

Suddenly the pamphlet blares out the question, "But who invented physics? Who made the bank deposits of coal and zinc and iron and uranium inside the earth? Nobody. It was just another priceless accident."

The writer concludes, "The human heart will beat for seventy or eighty years without faltering. How does it get sufficient rest be-

[1]Concordia Publishing House, 3558 South Jefferson Avenue, Saint Louis, Missouri.

Cram Course for Eternity

tween beats? Who gave the human tongue flexibility to form words and a brain to understand them, but denied it to all the animals? It's all accidental? There is no God? That's what some people say."

And how foolish these people are. Most make their godless declarations without thinking twice. Many even change their minds in later years. History declares that Sir Francis Newport, Voltaire, Tom Paine, David Hume, Altamont, Ethan Allen, and Thomas Hobbes—all outspoken unbelievers—cried out for God's mercy in their final moments. (Funny, isn't it?)

So let me encourage you to re-evaluate your opinion if you cannot accept the idea of God. Stop for a moment and honestly consider the evidence. Be open minded in the matter. It could well be the beginning of a mind-bending, life-changing experience that leads to total peace.

Cram Course for Eternity

What's Your Opinion?

Answer each question with statements of less than ten words each.

1. Give a simple definition of God.

2. List one basic reason for believing in God.

3. According to the Scriptures on the next page, why should we believe in God?

Cram Course for Eternity

The Bible Says . . .

"Only a fool would say to himself, 'There is no God.' And why does he say it? Because of his wicked heart, his dark and evil deeds. His life is corroded with sin" (PSALM 53:1).

"The Heavens are telling the glory of God; they are a marvelous display of his craftsmanship. Day and night they keep on telling about God. Without a sound or word, silent in the skies, their message reaches out to the world" (PSALM 19:1).

"Before anything else existed there was Christ, with God. He has always been alive and is himself God. He created everything there is—nothing exists that he didn't make" (JOHN 1:1).

"Christ is the exact likeness of the unseen God. He existed before God made anything at all . . . Christ himself is the Creator who made everything in heaven and earth. . . . He was before all else began and it is his power that holds everything together" (COLOSSIANS 1:15-17).

COMING UP NEXT . . .
The Truth About Jesus Christ!

the
son
factor

Hypothesis Three—True happiness in life, real peace, and the promise of eternal life, can be found only in accepting God's Son, Jesus Christ, as your personal Savior.

Cram Course for Eternity

Jesus Christ! That name sure is attracting attention these days. We used to hear it most frequently in cursing. And though people continue to use it in this regard, the name "Jesus" is being voiced more than ever by people finding life in that name.

The name Jesus has outlived all names over the past two thousand years. In fact, Napoleon once said, "I marvel that whereas the ambitious dreams of myself, Caesar and Alexander should have vanished into thin air, a Judean peasant, Jesus, should be able to stretch His hands across the centuries and control the destinies of men and nations."

That's my Jesus! He isn't just a mythical god who offers me fairy-tale hope. He is real. He is life. One of Christ's choice apostles simply said, "He is God's message of Life" (1 John 1:1). After receiving Him as king of my life I found each day packed with the big three of human experience—joy, peace, and power to meet daily challenges. Look at each of these a moment.

First, Jesus provides *joy*. This inward joy can hardly be described. I can only explain it with help of a simple story I heard recently. A father asked a little child why she liked her Sunday school teacher so much. She answered, "Because her eyes twinkle like she's laughing inside all the time." Quite simply, in Jesus I keep laughing inside all the time. Jesus is joy.

Cram Course for Eternity

Then, Jesus provides peace. Many years ago, in Southern Mexico, Bible translators searched for a word to use for "peace" in the Chol Indian language. They had no such word. Then, the translators discovered an expression that fit perfectly. It was "a quiet heart." These Indians don't say of Jesus that He "is our way of peace" (Ephesians 2:14). They say He "is our road to a quiet heart." And this is exactly what Jesus gives those who receive Him. Jesus is peace.

Last, Jesus provides power. A prominent New York physicist declares, "There is enough atomic energy in the body of one man to destroy the city of New York." And no doubt this is true. But let me describe a greater power. It is the tremendous power given to the believer in Christ who draws daily from God's supply house of spiritual energy. You see, Jesus is power.

There is power to take youth off drugs. There is power to mend broken homes. There is power to love people of all races. There is power to heal wounded humanity. And most of all, there is power to clean up the inner man.

How can we procure this power? How do we secure this peace and joy? It all comes as part of the Jesus life. And we gain this life only by coming to Christ in prayer, asking Him to enter our spiritual hearts. It's really quite simple, though many make it sound so

Cram Course for Eternity

mystical. It's all just a matter of making a decision to receive Christ as Lord of our life. To make Him Lord we must renounce our past and declare Christ King of our "now." This act is called repentance, which is the act of turning around and heading the other direction. We once lived in sin, having our own way about things. Now, with Christ's grace and help, we turn around. This is accepting Jesus as Lord.

When we accept Christ as Lord He automatically becomes our Savior. He saves us from a hopeless future after death (commonly called hell) and gives us eternal life (or heaven). And it happens in an instant. The Bible calls this being "born again." You can experience Jesus now! Why not stop momentarily and make your reservation for Eternity now? It will only take a sincere prayer of commitment.

> *Jesus . . . I come to You realizing I have failed to live in You. You have not been the King of my life and I wish You to be. I choose You as my Lord and Savior. I will live in You. It is in Your name I ask this,*
>   *Amen.*

Cram Course for Eternity

What's Your Opinion?

The Bible says that we can become true Christians if we confess our sins and believe in Christ as our Savior. With this in mind, write a prayer of confession, asking Christ to come into your life. Use your own words and expressions.

Dear Jesus,

Signed _____

Cram Course for Eternity

The Bible Says . . .

"And what is it that God has said? That he has given us eternal life, and that this life is in his Son. So whoever has God's Son has life; whoever does not have his Son, does not have life" (1 JOHN 5:11).

"When someone becomes a Christian he becomes a brand new person inside. He is not the same any more. A new life has begun! For God took the sinless Christ and poured into him our sins. Then, in exchange, he poured God's goodness into us" (2 CORINTHIANS 5:17 & 21).

"When you obey me you are living in my love, just as I obey my Father and live in his love. I have told you this so that you will be filled with my joy. Yes, your cup of joy will overflow!" (JOHN 15:10, 11).

"I have told you all this so that you will have peace of heart and mind. Here on earth you will have many trials and sorrows; but cheer up, for I have overcome the world" (JOHN 16:33).

COMING UP NEXT . . .
Our Source of Spiritual Power

the spirit factor

Hypothesis Four—The Bible clearly teaches we can be filled with the Holy Spirit, Who gives us added strength and power to live an overcoming life.

Cram Course for Eternity

Let me take you, a moment, back some nineteen hundred and fifty years in history. It is exactly forty days after the resurrection of Christ. Jesus is standing on top of a mountain ready to return to His Father in heaven. Five hundred disciples are standing nearby in fear, wondering how they can possibly survive without Jesus there in the flesh.

Christ, however, makes it plain He will give these followers a new power. He tells those present that another Comforter (power source) will enter them soon. He promises power to help tell the world about Himself and that this power would come by the Holy Spirit.

Our Lord further instructs the company to return to Jerusalem to wait for this power. And some did, though 380 somehow became distracted along the way. (The Bible reports that only 120 showed up for the amazing revival of Pentecost.)

Unfortunately, it seems we have on our hands a similar trend today. Some who find Christ as Lord and Savior never realize how much more waits for those filled to overflowing with His Spirit. Many have never been told they, too, can experience the Holy Spirit just like those disciples of the early church.

How can we receive this baptism? There are three basics to consider in answering

Cram Course for Eternity

this question. First, *we must pray for the Baptism in the Holy Spirit.* The Bible says, "Don't you realize that your heavenly Father will . . . give the Holy Spirit to those who ask for him?" (Luke 11:13). Asking, of course, is synonymous with prayer. Thus, we must pray.

Next, *we must be obedient to God in order to receive this baptism in the Holy Spirit.* Scripture says, "And we are witnesses of these things, and so is the Holy Spirit, who is given by God to all who obey him" (Acts 5:32). Thus we must first obey God's command to "believe on the Lord Jesus Christ" before we can receive the baptism of the Holy Spirit.

Third, *we must have faith to receive the baptism in the Holy Spirit.* The apostle Paul penned, "All of us as Christians can have the promised Holy Spirit through this faith" (Galatians 3:14). Thus the third basic is faith in the promise.

What can we expect if all three of these necessities are fulfilled? For one, we will suddenly sense the majesty of God as never before. A deep, intense love for Christ will come over us. In some instances it may affect our physical beings in a striking way. Remember, people thought the early disciples were actually drunk when they were baptised in the Spirit (See Acts, chapter 2.)

Cram Course for Eternity

We should also point out that a new language (or tongue) came upon those filled with the Spirit in the early church. Pat Boone, popular entertainer and leader in the charismatic movement, refers to this as his "prayer language" because it comes from the heart. Other recent converts to Christ, such as Johnny Cash, tell how precious it is to pray and sing in their heavenly language. In my home city, the capital of California, a high-level member of Governor Reagan's cabinet has led scores of people to this experience. He has frequently shared with me the validity of these baptisms.

I personally received this extra love-gift from God one night in prayer. Suddenly I started telling God I loved Him in a language that flowed from my heart. It was new and fresh. It has stayed with me over the years. It is more beautiful today than ever. Often I even find myself singing new melodies in this language.

Great leaders of the Church have shared similar testimony. Charles Finney, the renowned revival preacher of a century ago, told of his baptism, "I wept aloud with joy and love; and I do not know, but I should say I literally bellowed the unutterable gushings of my heart."

I encourage you to ask God, quietly and sincerely, for this rich experience. Then, simply receive it. You, too, will begin to

Cram Course for Eternity

communicate with God in a personal prayer language. And be certain not to let anyone deprive you of this promised gift. If someone discourages you from seeking this baptism, read the book of Acts in your Bible, and you will become convinced of its validity.

What's Your Opinion?

We have just finished reading about the three necessities to being filled with God's Spirit. Without looking back, can you remember the three?

Write the requirements in the spaces provided below.

1.

2.

3.

Check one of the following:

☐ I have met the three requirements and am waiting for the promise.

☐ I will strive to meet these requirements and then expect the promise.

Cram Course for Eternity

The Bible Says . . .

"And I will give you a new heart—I will give you new and right desires—and put a new spirit within you. I will take out your stony hearts of sin and give you new hearts of love. And I will put my Spirit within you so that you will obey my laws and do whatever I command" (EZEKIEL 36:26-27).

"But when the Holy Spirit has come upon you, you will receive power to testify about me with great effect, to the people in Jerusalem, throughout Judea, in Samaria, and to the ends of the earth, about my death and resurrection" (ACTS 1:8).

"And everyone present was filled with the Holy Spirit and began speaking in languages they didn't know, for the Holy Spirit gave them this ability" (ACTS 2:4).

"When the Holy Spirit controls our lives he will produce this kind of fruit in us: love, joy, peace, patience, kindness, goodness, faithfulness, gentleness, and self-control. . . . if we are living now by the Holy Spirit's power, let us follow the Holy Spirit's leading in every part of our lives" (GALATIANS 5:22 and 25).

COMING UP NEXT
Where We Can Find Real Truth!

the truth factor

Hypothesis Five—The Bible is the infallible Word of God, and thereby contains absolute truth for those who read it under the direction of God's Spirit.

Cram Course for Eternity

George Washington Carver was one of the most brilliant men who ever lived. But I consider him brilliant for much more than his mere scientific genius. Carver, in my opinion, excelled because of his love for the Bible. And this love of Scripture showed up in his work.

Take, for example, one memorable incident. For years Carver encouraged the black people of the south to plant crops besides cotton. Too often, a failure with the cotton crop left the people penniless.

Carver finally persuaded his people to plant peanuts. But before long they raised more peanuts then the people could possibly use. So Carver sought God's assistance in the matter. It wasn't long before he discovered how to make medicines, oils, dyes, varnishes, and scores of other items from the peanut.

Then one day Carver was invited to testify before a Senate sub-committee concerning his success with the peanut. At one point in the session he was asked, "How did you learn all these things about the peanut?" "From an old book," came Carver's reply.

The chairman queried, "What book, Mr. Carver?" Unashamedly the aging scientist answered, "The Bible." To this the committee chairman responded, "You mean to tell me your Bible talks about peanuts?"

"No," answered Dr. Carver, "but the

Cram Course for Eternity

Bible tells me about God Who made the peanut. So I just asked Him to show me what to do with His peanut, and He did."

George Washington Carver had learned a lesson we should likewise learn. The Bible can answer any question of life if we are willing to read it consistently. But we must make an effort to read and experience it.

So why not give yourself to a fresh and invigorating study of the Bible? Purchase a modern translation of the Bible and begin reading it daily. I recommend *The Living Bible* which is the translation quoted throughout *Cram Course for Eternity*. You can order your copy at any religious bookstore. (The publisher is Tyndale).

Make certain to mark your Bible when reading it. Enroll yourself in your own "College of the Word" and start studying for your finals. Memorize Scripture often. I recently read of a former black panther who found Christ and has now memorized almost the entire New Testament. If you play the guitar or are musically inclined, set scriptures to music. Write your own Bible songs. In doing this you are learning to live in the Word. (See the back of this booklet for a suggested year's study of the Bible.)

One excellent way to read the Bible is to start in the first book of the New Testament, Matthew, and read a portion daily. Read until you come to a verse that seems to leap

Cram Course for Eternity

from the page. Consider that your thought-for-the-day. Circle or underline it and write the date beside it. Stop reading there and begin at the same verse tomorrow. Some days you may read an entire chapter before your verse leaps out at you. Other days you may read only a few verses. But no matter what method you choose, I predict you will thoroughly enjoy your study of the Bible. Remember, ask the Holy Spirit for His help to understand what the Bible says. He guides us "into all truth" (John 16:13).

Oh yes, one more thing. I encourage newly converted youth (and adults) to start small "Bible studies" at home or school. If you are a new Christian, seek out another Christian on your campus or in your neighborhood; one who will meet with you each week to share in the Word. This will help you grow in the Book of truth God has given man as a standard for productive living.

Cram Course for Eternity

What's Your Opinion?

Go to the next page and carefully read the Bible verses listed.

Then, write seven facts you glean from these verses about the Bible. Make each statement short and to the point.

1. _____

2. _____

3. _____

4. _____

5. _____

6. _____

7. _____

Cram Course for Eternity

The Bible Says . . .

"The whole Bible was given to us by inspiration from God and is useful to teach us what is true and to make us realize what is wrong in our lives; it straightens us out and helps us do what is right" (TIMOTHY 3:16).

"For whatever God says to us is full of living power: it is sharper than the sharpest dagger, cutting swift and deep into our innermost thoughts and desires with all their parts, exposing us for what we really are" (HEBREWS 4:12).

"God's laws are pure, eternal, just. They are more desirable than gold. They are sweeter than honey dripping from a honeycomb. For they warn us away from harm and give success to those who obey them" (PSALMS 19:9-11).

"Constantly remind the people about these laws, and you yourselves must think about them every day and every night so that you will be sure to obey all of them. For only then will you succeed" (JOSHUA 1:8).

COMING UP NEXT
The Importance of Total Commitment!

the lordship factor

Hypothesis Six—Christ plainly taught, as does all of New Testament Scripture, that we must allow Him to be total Lord of our lives in daily obedience. This is the Lordship factor in our experience.

Cram Course for Eternity

From time to time, attending church becomes the social thing to do, and churches experience a dramatic upsurge in attendance. A few years back, spiritual revolution even hit the streets. We read of thousands of so-called "Jesus Freaks" who left "the drug trip" to "turn on" to Jesus.

Now let me be frank and honest. When things like this occur, some of these folk are genuinely converted to Christ. They have honestly made Him Lord. On the other hand, some have made only an outward confession of Christ when, in reality, they do not have inward possession by Christ. He is simply not their King and Commander.

I am reminded of a minister who was asked by an old friend how his church was getting on. During the conversation the friend questioned, "How many members do you have?" The minister replied, "About 1,000."

"Really?" asked the friend, adding, "and how many of them are active?"

To this the minister answered, "Oh, all of them are active. About two hundred are active for God and the balance for the devil."

How sad it is that so many new converts, and even some who have been around Christianity awhile, cannot seem to live the totally committed life. It's for this very reason that there are so many miserable Christians. It is truly painful to walk around (spiritually)

Cram Course for Eternity

with one foot in heaven and one in the world.

I like the way a former chaplain of the United States Senate, Peter Marshall, said it. He wrote, "We are too Christian really to enjoy sinning and too fond of sinning really to enjoy Christianity. Most of us know perfectly well what we ought to do; our trouble is that we do not want to do it."

Thus, our lesson here is simple. We must renounce our former hang-ups—with the help of God—and walk away from them. In turn, we must become totally obedient to Christ, and all He taught. This obedience might be termed the "Lordship of Christ." It is sometimes referred to as holiness.

In what areas should we be obedient? For one thing, we must read the Bible often. This we stressed in our last chapter. Also, we must pray daily; a subject we will discuss in the next section. But we could also cite such necessary acts of obedience as water baptism. This is simply an outward act (to the world) showing we have been cleansed within. The Bible teaches we are to repent, or turn from sin, and be baptised. I also believe we should attend church on a regular basis if we desire to be truly obedient. The Bible tells us not to neglect our church meetings.

This entire subject of the Lordship of Christ might be termed "continuance." This

Cram Course for Eternity

means that after we receive Christ as Savior we do not stop there. Rather, we daily allow Him to be Lord of all our decisions. And just how do we gain strength for this? We certainly cannot find it in ourselves. It comes from above.

Let me illustrate with a lesson from nature. Have you ever gazed upon a giant redwood? I have sat beneath redwood trees that reach heights of 300 feet here in California. How do they draw water to their leaves? Botanists tell us this process is not accomplished by pressure from the roots. Rather, it is done by pull from above.

So the lesson, applied to the spiritual, is clear. To grow taller, we must reach higher. Jesus will pull you from above. He is our strength. In Christ we grow.

Cram Course for Eternity

What's Your Opinion?

An acrostic involves taking a word and using each letter to form a number of new words, each describing the original word. An acrostic for SIN might be . . .

S elfishness
I ndifference
N eglect

Write an acrostic that explains Christ as our Lord. Use the four letters in the word Lord.

L

O

R

D

Cram Course for Eternity

The Bible Says . . .

"For the eyes of the Lord search back and forth across the whole earth, looking for people whose hearts are perfect toward him, so that he can show his great power in helping them" (2 CHRONICLES 16:9).

"Take your share of suffering as a good soldier of Jesus Christ, just as I do, and as Christ's soldier do not let yourself become tied up in worldly affairs, for then you cannot satisfy the one who has enlisted you in his army" (2 TIMOTHY 2:3,4).

"It is true that I am an ordinary, weak human being, but I don't use human plans and methods to win my battles. I use God's mighty weapons, not those made by men, to knock down the devil's strongholds" (2 CORINTHIANS 10:3,4).

"Having such great promises as these, dear friends, let us turn away from everything wrong, whether of body or spirit, and purify ourselves, living in the wholesome fear of God, giving ourselves to him alone" (2 CORINTHIANS 7:1).

COMING UP NEXT . . .
How To Communicate With God

the prayer factor

Hypothesis Seven—It is a Bible premise that God will hear the prayers Christians pray, and further, that daily prayer is essential if we wish to survive spiritually.

Cram Course for Eternity

We come, now, to a crucial part of our time together. It concerns communication with God Himself. This is most commonly called prayer. And prayer works. Dwight David Eisenhower, one of America's great presidents, said, "Prayer gives you the courage to make the decision you must make in a crisis and then the confidence to leave the results to a higher power."

As you press forward in your Christian experience, you will sometimes collide with problems that seem insurmountable. You will need outside help to get through. Where do you gain this help? From God, through prayer. You see, prayer is power. Prayer links us with our powerful Creator. I like the description a great scientist gives, "Prayer is the mightiest force in the universe."

Of course, there are several things we should learn about true prayer. These conditions are important to understand if we desire answers to our prayers. Study these with me a moment. And please note they are all fully supported by the Bible.

First, we must not allow sin in our lives. Sin hinders prayer. In Psalms the writer says, "I cried to him for help, with praises ready on my tongue. He would not have listened if I had not confessed my sins" (Psalm 66:17-18). Therefore, we cannot allow sin in our lives if we wish to have our prayers answered. Confession of all known sins opens

Cram Course for Eternity

the gateway to God.

Second, we must use the name of Jesus as our complete basis for prayer. Quite simply, we are asking God to answer our prayer with the name of His Son standing behind that prayer. Jesus himself said, "Yes, ask *anything,* using my name, and I will do it" (John 14:14).

Third, we must decide before we pray to let God do as He desires concerning a given matter. This is generally referred to as "having God's will." And those who pray must learn the necessity of letting God answer our prayer as He sees fit. Sometimes we may find ourselves waiting at great length for an answer. This is often because He sees the wait as needful. The Bible says, "We are sure of this, that he will listen to us whenever we ask him for anything *in line with His will*" (1 John 5:14).

Never forget these important factors in prayer. We must confess our sins and come to God with a clean heart. We must pray in the name of Jesus. And we must desire God's will in each instance, no matter what we may wish personally.

What else can be said concerning prayer? Perhaps I should mention that God answers prayer in three basic ways. He may say *yes* or *no,* or even *wait.* Thus, the most important thing we can do in prayer is let God be God and reserve Him the right to choose what He

Cram Course for Eternity

wishes concerning a particular prayer.

Let me explain with an account from my own experience that may prove profitable. When I was twenty-five, I found myself suffering from a severe throat condition. Being a young minister I wanted very much to continue my speaking ministry for Jesus. But little improvement came for many months. I had to leave my pulpit. The throat grew progressively worse. And meanwhile, everyone I knew was praying for me. Old people, young people, children, ministers, wealthy businessmen—everyone who knew me was praying. But for months nothing happened, except inside my human spirit. God was teaching me patience and the real importance of prayer. It was during those long lonesome months that He led me into a writing ministry. God taught me to preach with the pen. So what I thought was an extremely painful experience became one of my greatest victories in life. Why? Because God decided to wait in giving me my answer. And in waiting I gained a rich reward.

So let God be God in your life, and in your prayers. Commit everything to Him. Let no one destroy the faith you have found in Christ. Stand up for it at all cost. Refuse to run when friends mock or ridicule your decision to follow Christ. Instead, stay in the battle and lead those very friends to the point they, too, will embrace Jesus as their Lord.

Cram Course for Eternity

What's Your Opinion?

David Livingstone, the great African missionary, had the habit of writing a prayer, once each year, for the following year. Write a prayer to God and list your desires for next year.

Dear God,

Date _____

Signed _____

Cram Course for Eternity

The Bible Says . . .

"Pray all the time. Ask God for anything in line with the Holy Spirit's wishes. Plead with him, reminding him of your needs, and keep praying earnestly for all Christians everywhere" (EPHESIANS 6:18).

"Pray much for others: plead for God's mercy upon them; give thanks for all he is going to do for them. Pray in this way for kings and all others who are in authority over us, or are in places of high responsibility so that we can live in peace and quietness, spending our time in godly living and thinking much about the Lord" (1 TIMOTHY 2:1,2).

"Listen to me! You can pray for anything and if you believe, you have it; it's yours! But when you are praying, first forgive anyone you are holding a grudge against, so that your Father in heaven will forgive your sins too" (MARK 11:24,25).

"Ask and you will be given what you ask for. Seek, and you will find. Knock, and the door will be opened. For everyone who asks, receives. Anyone who seeks, finds. If only you will knock, the door will open" (MATTHEW 7:7,8).

Welcome to

THE COLLEGE

of the

WORD

Cram Course for Eternity

Fifty-Two Weeks in the College of the Word

Welcome to the College of the Word. You have just enrolled for one year, starting today. There is only one textbook, the Bible. And though you may read other good Christian literature, the Bible must remain your key source of material. You are to read, study, analyze, and digest each assigned chapter for a particular week. Read the chapter through during the first two days of that week. Then re-read it several verses at a time, writing your own notes. Pick the key words in each verse and do a word study. Write poetry based on one verse of that chapter, if you wish. Or, if you are musically inclined, compose music for a verse in that chapter. Also, try to memorize at least one verse from that chapter. You have seven full days to accomplish this. It will take much self-discipline. And you will have to grade yourself. Put a check before each assigned chapter when you have completed a week-long study of that material. Of course, you will need a good Bible. We have already recommended *The Living Bible*, though any good translation will do. The important thing is to start at once. Here is your fifty-two week plan.

Cram Course for Eternity

Check when completed—Study a chapter each week
- ☐ 1. Study Matthew 5
  IMPORTANT TEACHINGS OF JESUS
- ☐ 2. Study Mark 16
  CHRIST'S FINAL INSTRUCTIONS TO DISCIPLES
- ☐ 3. Study Luke 10
  MORE INSTRUCTIONS FROM JESUS
- ☐ 4. Study John 15
  LIVING IN JESUS
- ☐ 5. Study Acts 2
  PENTECOST AND ITS POWER
- ☐ 6. Study Romans 8
  THE WALK IN GOD'S SPIRIT
- ☐ 7. Study 1 Corinthians 13
  THE LOVE CHAPTER
- ☐ 8. Study 2 Corinthians 12
  THE GRACE CHAPTER
- ☐ 9. Study Galatians 5
  THE FRUITS OF THE SPIRIT
- ☐ 10. Study Ephesians 6
  GOD'S ARMOR FOR BATTLE
- ☐ 11. Study Philippians 4
  A STUDY OF THE PURE LIFE
- ☐ 12. Study Colossians 3
  THINGS IN LIFE TO SEEK
- ☐ 13. Study 1 Thessalonians 5
  BETWEEN NOW AND CHRIST'S COMING
- ☐ 14. Study 2 Thessalonians 2
  ABOUT THE DAY OF THE LORD
- ☐ 15. Study 1 Timothy 6
  LEARNING TO BE CONTENT
- ☐ 16. Study 2 Timothy 2
  DEVELOPING AS A JESUS SOLDIER
- ☐ 17. Study Titus 3
  LESSONS IN CHRIST'S GRACE AND MERCY
- ☐ 18. Study Philemon (23 verses)
  LOVE OF MASTER TO SERVANT
- ☐ 19. Study Hebrews 11
  THE FAITH CHAPTER

Cram Course for Eternity

- [ ] 20. Study James 2
  FAITH AND WORKS COMBINED
- [ ] 21. Study 1 Peter 2
  GROWING IN GOD'S WORD
- [ ] 22. Study 2 Peter 1
  LESSONS IN SPIRITUAL ADDITION
- [ ] 23. Study 1 John 4
  LESSONS IN LOVE
- [ ] 24. Study 2 John (13 verses)
  REJECTING FALSE DOCTRINE
- [ ] 25. Study 3 John (14 verses)
  SOUL PROSPERITY
- [ ] 26. Study Jude (25 verses)
  CONTENDING FOR THE FAITH
- [ ] 27. Study Revelation 21
  OUR FUTURE HOME IN HEAVEN
- [ ] 28. Study Genesis 3
  FIRST TEMPTATION AND SIN
- [ ] 29. Study Exodus 20
  THE TEN COMMANDMENTS
- [ ] 30. Study Leviticus 26
  THE "IF" CLAUSE FOR GOD'S BLESSINGS
- [ ] 31. Study Numbers 13
  THE POSITIVE VS. THE NEGATIVE
- [ ] 32. Study Numbers 2
  IT IS NOW TIME TO MOVE FORWARD
- [ ] 33. Study Joshua 3
  GOD WILL DO WONDERS
- [ ] 34. Study Judges 6
  THE STORY OF GIDEON
- [ ] 35. Study 1 Samuel 15
  THE NEED FOR OBEDIENCE
- [ ] 36. Study 2 Samuel 12
  WE REAP WHAT IS SOWED
- [ ] 37. Study 1 Kings 19
  THE QUIET VOICE OF GOD
- [ ] 38. Study 2 Kings 2
  THE DOUBLE PORTION OF THE SPIRIT
- [ ] 39. Study 1 Chronicles 14
  GOD PREPARES A MIRACLE ARMY

Cram Course for Eternity

- ☐ 40. Study 2 Chronicles 5
   THE GLORY IN THE TEMPLE
- ☐ 41. Study Ezra 10
   A PLEDGE TO REAL HOLINESS
- ☐ 42. Study Nehemiah 2
   LET US BUILD FOR GOD
- ☐ 43. Study Job 1
   A LESSON IN AMAZING FAITH
- ☐ 44. Study Psalm 119
   THE TRUTH ABOUT THE TRUTH
- ☐ 45. Study Proverbs 3
   TRUSTING GOD, AND HIS WORD
- ☐ 46. Study Isaiah 62
   HERE COME "THE HOLY PEOPLE"
- ☐ 47. Study Jeremiah 1
   DON'T BE AFRAID OF PEOPLE
- ☐ 48. Study Lamentations 3
   LESSONS ON GOD'S COMPASSION
- ☐ 49. Study Ezekiel 37
   AN ARMY ON THE RISE
- ☐ 50. Study Daniel 6
   A LOOK AT A PRAYER HABIT
- ☐ 51. Study Joel 2
   SOME THINGS TO COME
- ☐ 52. Study Malachi 3
   LESSONS ON GIVING

SPECIAL NOTE: When you have completed this basic overview of the Bible, begin a systematic study of the entire Bible—book by book, chapter by chapter. It will revolutionize your life. After doing the above study use the following day by day Bible study guide for reading the Bible through in one year. This could be done simultaneously with the above study, or in your second year at the College of the Word.

Cram Course for Eternity

A Guide to Reading the Bible in a Year

January

1 Gen. 1-2
2 Gen. 3-5
3 Gen. 6-9
4 Gen. 10-11
5 Gen. 12-15
6 Gen. 16-19
7 Gen. 20-22
8 Gen. 23-26
9 Gen. 27-29
10 Gen. 30-32
11 Gen. 33-36
12 Gen. 37-39
13 Gen. 40-42
14 Gen. 43-46
15 Gen. 47-50
16 Ex. 1-4
17 Ex. 5-7
18 Ex. 8-10
19 Ex. 11-13
20 Ex. 14-17
21 Ex. 18-20
22 Ex. 21-24
23 Ex. 25-27
24 Ex. 28-31
25 Ex. 32-34
26 Ex. 35-37
27 Ex. 38-40
28 Lev. 1-4
29 Lev. 5-7
30 Lev. 8-10
31 Lev. 11-13

February

1 Lev. 14-16
2 Lev. 17-19
3 Lev. 20-23
4 Lev. 24-27
5 Num. 1-3
6 Num. 4-6
7 Num. 7-10
8 Num. 11-14
9 Num. 15-17
10 Num. 18-20
11 Num. 21-24
12 Num. 25-27
13 Num. 28-30
14 Num. 31-33
15 Num. 34-36
16 Dt. 1-3
17 Dt. 4-6
18 Dt. 7-9
19 Dt. 10-12
20 Dt. 13-16
21 Dt. 17-19
22 Dt. 20-22
23 Dt. 23-25
24 Dt. 26-28
25 Dt. 29-31
26 Dt. 32-34
27 Josh. 1-3
28 Josh 4-6

March

1 Josh. 7-9
2 Josh. 10-12
3 Josh. 13-15
4 Josh. 16-18
5 Josh. 19-21
6 Josh. 22-24
7 Judg. 1-4
8 Judg. 5-8
9 Judg. 9-12
10 Judg. 13-15
11 Judg. 16-18
12 Judg. 19-21
13 Ruth 1-4
14 1 Sam. 1-3
15 1 Sam. 4-7
16 1 Sam. 8-10
17 1 Sam. 11-13
18 1 Sam. 14-16
19 1 Sam. 17-20
20 1 Sam. 21-24
21 1 Sam. 25-28
22 1 Sam. 29-31
23 2 Sam. 1-4
24 2 Sam. 5-8
25 2 Sam. 9-12
26 2 Sam. 13-15
27 2 Sam. 16-18
28 2 Sam. 19-21
29 2 Sam. 22-24
30 1 Ki. 1-4
31 1 Ki. 5-7

April

1 1 Ki. 8-10
2 1 Ki. 11-13
3 1 Ki. 14-16
4 1 Ki. 17-19
5 1 Ki. 20-22
6 2 Ki. 1-3
7 2 Ki. 4-6
8 2 Ki. 7-10
9 2 Ki. 11-14
10 2 Ki. 15-17
11 2 Ki. 18-19
12 2 Ki. 20-21
13 2 Ki. 22-25
14 1 Chr. 1-3
15 1 Chr. 4-6
16 1 Chr. 7-9
17 1 Chr. 10-13
18 1 Chr. 14-16
19 1 Chr. 17-19
20 1 Chr. 20-23
21 1 Chr. 24-26
22 1 Chr. 27-29
23 2 Chr. 1-3
24 2 Chr. 4-6
25 2 Chr. 7-9
26 2 Chr. 10-13
27 2 Chr. 14-16
28 2 Chr. 17-19
29 2 Chr. 20-22
30 2 Chr. 23-25

May

1 2 Chr. 26-29
2 2 Chr. 30-32
3 2 Chr. 33-36
4 Ezra 1-4
5 Ezra 5-7
6 Ezra 8-10
7 Neh. 1-3
8 Neh. 4-6
9 Neh. 7-9
10 Neh. 10-13
11 Esther 1-3
12 Esther 4-7
13 Esther 8-10
14 Job 1-4
15 Job 5-7
16 Job 8-10
17 Job 11-13
18 Job 14-17
19 Job 18-20
20 Job 21-24
21 Job 25-27
22 Job 28-31
23 Job 32-34
24 Job 35-37
25 Job 38-42
26 Ps. 1-3
27 Ps. 4-6
28 Ps. 7-9
29 Ps. 10-12
30 Ps. 13-15
31 Ps. 16-18

June

1 Ps. 19-21
2 Ps. 22-24
3 Ps. 25-27
4 Ps. 28-30
5 Ps. 31-33
6 Ps. 34-36
7 Ps. 37-39
8 Ps. 40-42
9 Ps. 43-45
10 Ps. 46-48
11 Ps. 49-51
12 Ps. 52-54
13 Ps. 55-57
14 Ps. 58-60
15 Ps. 61-63
16 Ps. 64-66
17 Ps. 67-69
18 Ps. 70-72
19 Ps. 73-75
20 Ps. 76-78
21 Ps. 79-81
22 Ps. 82-84
23 Ps. 85-87
24 Ps. 88-90
25 Ps. 91-93
26 Ps. 94-96
27 Ps. 97-99
28 Ps. 100-102
29 Ps. 103-105
30 Ps. 106-108

July

1 Ps. 109-111
2 Ps. 112-114
3 Ps. 115-118

Cram Course for Eternity

4 Ps. 119
5 Ps. 120-123
6 Ps. 124-126
7 Ps. 127-129
8 Ps. 130-132
9 Ps. 133-135
10 Ps. 136-138
11 Ps. 139-141
12 Ps. 142-144
13 Ps. 145-147
14 Ps. 148-150
15 Pr. 1-3
16 Pr. 4-7
17 Pr. 8-11
18 Pr. 12-14
19 Pr. 15-18
20 Pr. 19-21
21 Pr. 22-24
22 Pr. 25-28
23 Pr. 29-31
24 Eccl. 1-3
25 Eccl. 4-6
26 Eccl. 7-9
27 Eccl. 10-12
28 Song 1-4
29 Song 5-8
30 Isa. 1-3
31 Isa. 4-6

August

1 Isa. 7-9
2 Isa. 10-12
3 Isa. 13-15
4 Isa. 16-18
5 Isa. 19-21
6 Isa. 22-24
7 Isa. 25-27
8 Isa. 28-30
9 Isa. 31-33
10 Isa. 34-36
11 Isa. 37-39
12 Isa. 40-42
13 Isa. 43-45
14 Isa. 46-48
15 Isa. 49-51
16 Isa. 52-54
17 Isa. 55-57
18 Isa. 58-60
19 Isa. 61-63
20 Isa. 64-66
21 Jer. 1-3
22 Jer. 4-7
23 Jer. 8-11
24 Jer. 12-16
25 Jer. 17-19
26 Jer. 20-22
27 Jer. 23-25
28 Jer. 26-29
29 Jer. 30-32
30 Jer. 33-36
31 Jer. 37-39

September

1 Jer. 40-42
2 Jer. 43-46
3 Jer. 47-49
4 Jer. 50-52
5 Lam. 1-5
6 Ezek. 1-3
7 Ezek. 4-7
8 Ezek. 8-11
9 Ezek. 12-14
10 Ezek. 15-18
11 Ezek. 19-21
12 Ezek. 22-24
13 Ezek. 25-27
14 Ezek. 28-30
15 Ezek. 31-33
16 Ezek. 34-36
17 Ezek. 37-39
18 Ezek. 40-42
19 Ezek. 43-45
20 Ezek. 46-48
21 Dan. 1-3
22 Dan. 4-6
23 Dan. 7-9
24 Dan. 10-12
25 Hos. 1-4
26 Hos. 5-7
27 Hos. 8-10
28 Hos. 11-14
29 Joel 1-3
30 Amos 1-3

October

1 Amos 4-6
2 Amos 7-9
3 Oba.-Jonah
4 Mic. 1-4
5 Mic. 5-7
6 Nah. 1-3
7 Hab. 1-3
8 Zeph. 1-3
9 Hag. 1-2
10 Zech. 1-5
11 Zech. 6-10
12 Zech. 11-14
13 Mal. 1-4
14 Mt. 1-4
15 Mt. 5-7
16 Mt. 8-11
17 Mt. 12-15
18 Mt. 16-19
19 Mt. 20-22
20 Mt. 23-25
21 Mt. 26-28
22 Mk. 1-3
23 Mk. 4-6
24 Mk. 7-10
25 Mk. 11-13
26 Mk. 14-16
27 Lk. 1-3
28 Lk. 4-6
29 Lk. 7-9
30 Lk. 10-13
31 Lk. 14-17

November

1 Lk. 18-21
2 Lk. 22-24
3 Jn. 1-3
4 Jn. 4-6
5 Jn. 7-10
6 Jn. 11-13
7 Jn. 14-17
8 Jn. 18-21
9 Acts 1-2
10 Acts 3-5
11 Acts 6-9
12 Acts 10-12
13 Acts 13-14
14 Acts 15-18
15 Acts 19-20
16 Acts 21-22
17 Acts 23-25
18 Acts 26-28
19 Rom. 1-4
20 Rom. 5-8
21 Rom. 9-11
22 Rom. 12-16
23 1 Cor. 1-4
24 1 Cor. 5-8
25 1 Cor. 9-12
26 1 Cor. 13-16
27 2 Cor. 1-3
28 2 Cor. 4-6
29 2 Cor. 7-9
30 2 Cor. 10-13

December

1 Gal. 1-3
2 Gal. 4-6
3 Eph. 1-3
4 Eph. 4-6
5 Phil. 1-4
6 Col. 1-4
7 1 Th. 1-5
8 2 Th. 1-3
9 1 Tim. 1-3
10 1 Tim. 4-6
11 2 Tim. 1-4
12 Tit. - Ph'm
13 Heb. 1-4
14 Heb. 5-7
15 Heb. 8-10
16 Heb. 11-13
17 Jas. 1-2
18 Jas. 3-5
19 1 Pet. 1-2
20 1 Pet. 3-5
21 2 Pet. 1-3
22 1 Jn. 1-2
23 1 Jn. 3-5
24 2 Jn.,3 Jn., Jude
25 Rev. 1-3
26 Rev. 4-5
27 Rev. 6-9
28 Rev. 10-13
29 Rev. 14-16
30 Rev. 17-18
31 Rev. 19-22

Cram Course for Eternity

**WHEREVER PAPERBACKS ARE SOLD
OR USE THIS COUPON**

Whitaker House
504 LAUREL DRIVE
MONROEVILLE, PA 15146

SEND INSPIRATIONAL BOOKS
LISTED BELOW

Title Price ☐ Send Complete Catalog

_____ _____
_____ _____
_____ _____
_____ _____
_____ _____
_____ _____
_____ _____

Name _____

Street _____

City _____ State _____ Zip _____

Suggested Inspirational Paperback Books

FACE UP WITH A MIRACLE
by Don Basham — $1.25

This is a fascinating book about God the Holy Spirit bringing a new dimension into the lives of twentieth-century Christians. It is filled with experiences that testify to a God of miracles being unleashed in our lives right now.

THE PURPLE PIG AND OTHER MIRACLES
by Dick Eastman — $1.50

Hidden away in a rambling, wood-frame house on "O" Street in Sacramento, there is a special underground room where Bible-believing Christians pray twenty-four hours a day, seven days a week. Miracles? They happen all the time. And the prayer power is spreading...

A SCRIPTURAL OUTLINE OF THE BAPTISM IN THE HOLY SPIRIT
by George and Harriet Gillies — 60c

Here is a very brief and simple outline of the baptism in the Holy Spirit, with numerous references under each point. This handy little booklet is a good reference for any question you might have concerning this subject.

A HANDBOOK ON HOLY SPIRIT BAPTISM
by Don Basham — $1.25

Questions and answers on the baptism in the Holy Spirit and speaking in tongues. The book is in great demand, and answers many important questions from within the contemporary Christian church.

HE SPOKE, AND I WAS STRENGTHENED
by Dick Mills — $1.25

An easy-to-read devotional of 52 prophetic scripturally-based messages directed to the businessman, the perfectionist, the bereaved, the lonely, the ambitious and many more.

Cram Course for Eternity

SEVEN TIMES AROUND
by Bob and Ruth McKee $1.25
A Christian growth story of a family who receives the baptism in the Holy Spirit and then applies this new experience to solve the family's distressing, but frequently humorous problems.

LET GO!
by Fenelon 95c
Jesus promised a life full of joy and peace. Why then are so many Christians struggling to attain the qualities that Christ said belonged to the child of God? Fenelon speaks firmly—but lovingly—to those whose lives have been an up hill battle. Don't miss this one.

VISIONS BEYOND THE VEIL
by H. A. Baker $1.25
Beggar children who heard the Gospel at a rescue mission in China, received a powerful visitation of the Holy Spirit, during which they saw visions of Heaven and Christ which cannot be explained away. A new revised edition.

DEAR DAD, THIS IS TO ANNOUNCE MY DEATH by Ric Kast $1.25
The story of how rock music, drugs and alcohol lead a youth to commit suicide. While Ric waits out the last moments of life, Jesus Christ rescues him from death and gives him a new life.

GATEWAY TO POWER
by Wesley Smith $1.25
From the boredom of day after day routine and lonely nights of meaningless activity, Wes Smith was caught up into a life of miracles. Dramatic healings, remarkable financial assistance, and exciting escapes from dangerous situations have become part of his life.

SIGI AND I
by Gwen Schmidt $1.25

The intriguing narration of how two women smuggled Bibles and supplies to Christians behind the Iron Curtain. An impressive account of their simple faith in following the Holy Spirit.

SPIRITUAL POWER
by Don Basham $1.25

Over 100 received new spiritual power after hearing the author give this important message. The book deals with such topics as the baptism as a second experience, the primary evidence of the baptism, and tongues and the "Chronic Seeker."

THE LAST CHAPTER
by A. W. Rasmussen $1.45

An absorbing narrative based on the author's own experience, in the charismatic renewal around the world. He presents many fresh insights on fasting, church discipline and Christ's Second Coming.

A HANDBOOK ON TONGUES, INTERPRETATION AND PROPHECY
by Don Basham $1.25

The second of Don Basham's Handbook series. Again set up in the convenient question and answer format, the book addresses itself to further questions on the Holy Spirit, especially the vocal gifts.